Contents

1	**From rock to soil**	**4**
1.1	Your rocky home	5
1.2	The three rock groups	6
1.3	Weathering	7
1.4	The rock cycle	8
1.5	The British Isles on their travels	9
1.6	Rock around the UK	10
1.7	Rock and landscapes	11
1.8	Soil … and you	12

2	**Living off Earth's resources**	**13**
2.1	Earth's natural resources	14
2.2	Water around the world	15
2.3	What have they done to Ogallala?	16
2.4	The growing water challenge	17
2.5	Soil … a precious resource	18
2.6	Desertification in the drylands	19
2.7	The fight against desertification	20
2.8	Oil for energy	21
2.9	Renewable sources of energy in the UK	22
2.10	Solar power around the world	23
2.11	But what about other species?	24

3	**Earning a living**	**25**
3.1	The UK at work	26
3.2	So where are the jobs?	27
3.3	The UK's changing employment structure	28
3.4	Change in and around Doncaster	29
3.5	Employment structure in other countries	30
3.6	Where did the UK's factory jobs go?	31
3.7	The clothing industry in Bangladesh	32
3.8	Working to bring you a mobile	33

4	**International development**	**34**
4.1	Rich world, poor world	35
4.2	So what is development?	36
4.3	Measuring and mapping development	37
4.4	Malawi: a developing country	38
4.5	Singapore: a developed country	39
4.6	How did the development gap grow? – part 1	40
4.7	How did the development gap grow? – part 2	41
4.8	Escaping from poverty	42
4.9	Putting an end to poverty	43

5	**Our restless planet**	**44**
5.1	A slice through Earth	45
5.2	Our cracked Earth	46
5.3	A closer look at plate movements	47
5.4	Earthquakes	48
5.5	An earthquake in Southwest China	49
5.6	Tsunami!	50
5.7	Volcanoes	51
5.8	Iceland: a country made by volcanoes	52
5.9	Why live in a danger zone?	53

6	**Russia**	**54**
6.1	Meet Russia	55
6.2	A little history	56
6.3	Russia's main physical features	57
6.4	Russia's climate zones and biomes	58
6.5	What about the people?	59
6.6	A tour of European Russia	60
6.7	Sakha: Russia's biggest region	61
6.8	So … how is Russia doing?	62

7	**The Middle East**	**63**
7.1	Introducing the Middle East	64
7.2	The Middle East: physical geography	65
7.3	The Middle East: climate zones and biomes	66
7.4	The people of the Middle East	67
7.5	A closer look at the Arabian Peninsula	68
7.6	Conflict in the Middle East	69
7.7	Israel and the State of Palestine	70

1 From rock to soil

pages 4–5

1 Look at the photograph below. In the boxes write down four things that you would like to find out about the feature shown in the image.

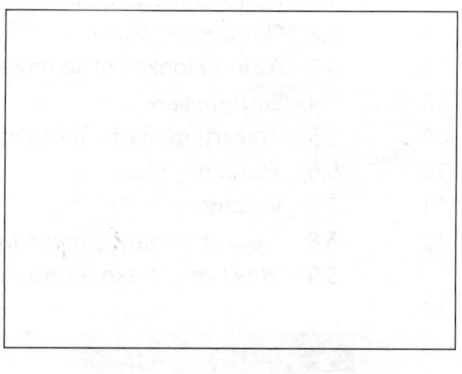

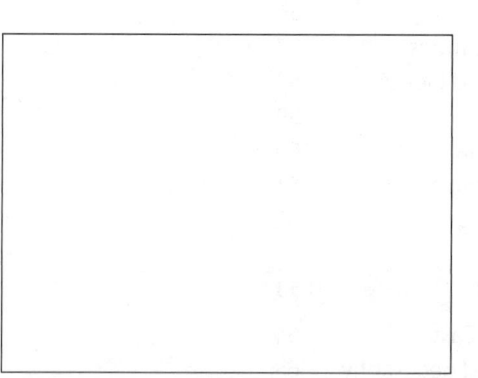

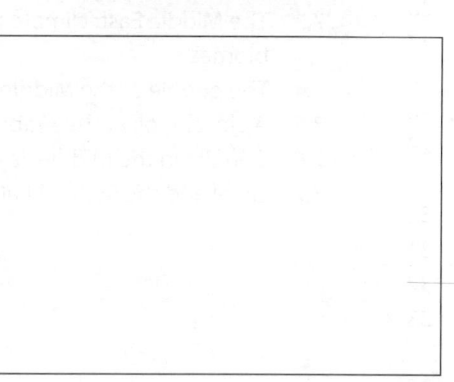

2 Imagine you are on top of the mountain. Write a tweet describing what you see and how you feel. Use as many adjectives as you can.

_____
_____
_____
_____

4 From rock to soil

4th edition

geog.3
workbook

< justin woolliscroft >

Name:

Class:

OXFORD

Great Clarendon Street, Oxford, OX2 6DP, United Kingdom

Oxford University Press is a department of the University of Oxford. It furthers the University's objective of excellence in research, scholarship, and education by publishing worldwide. Oxford is a registered trade mark of Oxford University Press in the UK and in certain other countries

© Oxford University Press 2015

Author: Justin Woolliscroft

The moral rights of the authors have been asserted

Database right Oxford University Press (maker)

First published 2006

New edition published 2009

This edition published 2015

All rights reserved. No part of this publication may be reproduced, stored in a retrieval system, or transmitted, in any form or by any means, without the prior permission in writing of Oxford University Press, or as expressly permitted by law, by licence or under terms agreed with the appropriate reprographics rights organization. Enquiries concerning reproduction outside the scope of the above should be sent to the Rights Department, Oxford University Press, at the address above.

You must not circulate this work in any other form and you must impose this same condition on any acquirer

British Library Cataloguing in Publication Data
Data available

ISBN 978-0-19-839307-8

10 9 8 7 6 5 4 3 2 1

Paper used in the production of this book is a natural, recyclable product made from wood grown in sustainable forests. The manufacturing process conforms to the environmental regulations of the country of origin.

Printed in Great Britain by Ashford Print and Publishing Services, Gosport.

Acknowledgements

The publisher would like to thank the following for permissions to use photographs and other copyright material:

Cover: (globe) Getty Images, (headphones) Maximus256/Shutterstock; **p4:** © Richard Newton/Alamy; **p7:** © Mark Richardson/Alamy; **p11:** VisitBritain/Matt Cant/Getty Images; **p17:** Logo usage with kind permission from WaterAid; WaterAid is a registered charity: England and Wales 288701, Scotland SC039479; **p18:** PhotoQuest/Getty Images; **P50:** (left) AFP/Getty Images; (middle left) AFP/Getty Images; (middle right) Associated Press; (right) Associated Press; **p55:** Holger Mette/iStockphoto; **p57:** © Images & Stories/Alamy; **p61:** Amos Chapple/Getty Images; **p63:** Ischmidt/Shutterstock

Artwork by Phoenix Photosetting.

Some pages or activities in this edition are based on material written by Anna King, Catherine Hurst, and Katherine James for the original edition.

Links to third party websites are provided by Oxford in good faith and for information only. Oxford disclaims any responsibility for the materials contained in any third party website referenced in this work.

Every effort has been made to contact copyright holders of material reproduced in this book. Any omissions will be rectified in subsequent printings if notice is given to the publisher.

1 Your rocky home

This is about the rocks that are beneath our feet.

Complete the crossword to show your knowledge of rocks. Use the information on pages 6–7 in the pupil book to help you.

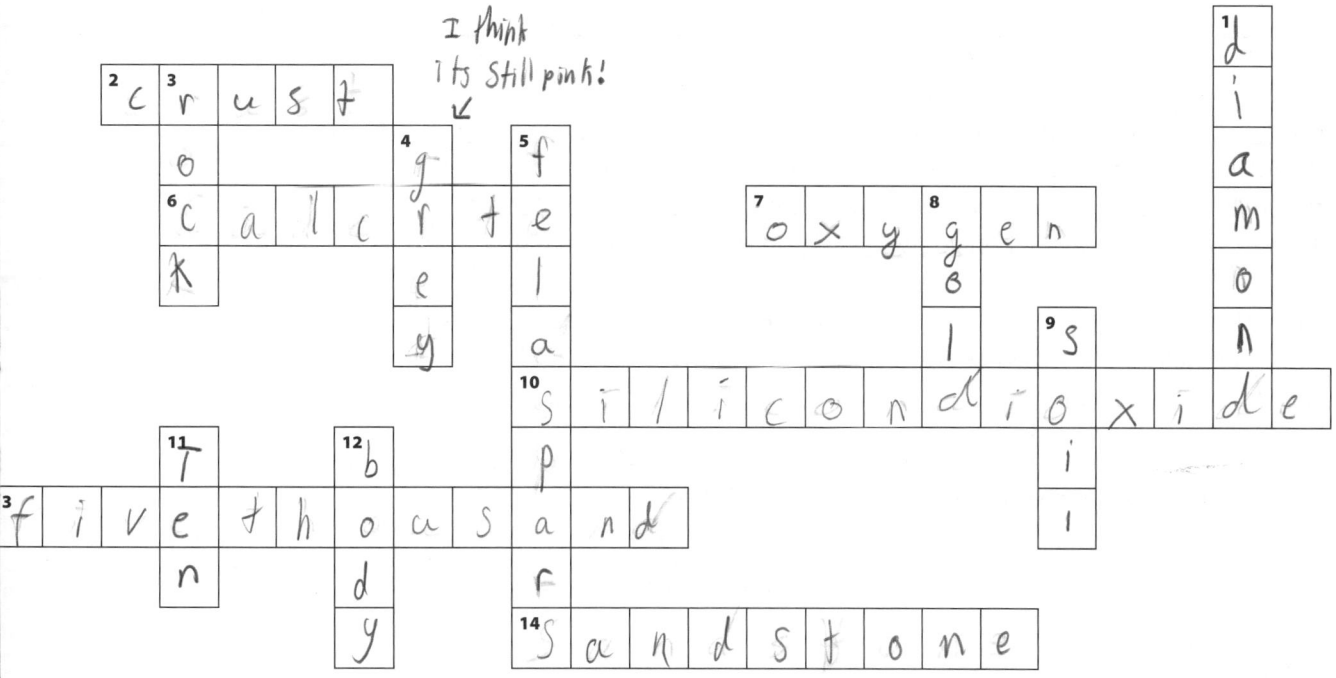

I think its still pink!

Clues

Across

2. The hard outer layer of the Earth
6. Another name for calcium carbonate
7. This gas is found in feldspars
10. Another name for quartz
13. The number of known minerals
14. This rock is mainly quartz. The crystals are very small

Down

1. A very precious stone found in rocks
3. A mixture of minerals
4. The colour of potassium feldspar
5. Made of silicon and oxygen
8. A precious metal found in rocks
9. The top layer of the Earth
11. The number of common minerals
12. Contains atoms of more than 61 elements

2. Go to the British Geological Survey's website. Find out what rocks lie beneath your feet and write a description of the geology of your area below.

_____
_____
_____
_____

From rock to soil 5

1.2 The three rock groups

This is about igneous rocks.

pages 8–9

1 Complete the sentences below. Use the words in the box to help you.

| lock | lava | slowly | melt | crystals | magma | hot | quickly |

Deep in the ground it is so __hot__ that minerals in the rock __melt__ giving a liquid called __magma__. The magma then often rises and cools. It may cool __slowly__ below ground and the minerals form large __crystals__ which __lock__ together forming rocks like granite. Some magma does reach the earth's surface, and spurts out of volcanoes as __lava__. This then cools __quickly__ to form rocks like basalt.

2 Igneous rock forms when rock melts, then cools and hardens once again. The elements that make up all rocks are never created or destroyed; instead they are constantly being recycled.

In the box below design a logo or symbol that could be used tell people this fact about rocks – the oldest recycling machine on the planet! Be as creative and inventive as you can!

6 From rock to soil

.3 Weathering

This is about weathering and how it shapes rocks.

pages 10–11

1. Lions are the kings of the jungle because of their raw power and strength; however, nothing can stop the weather!

Look at the sketch of the stone lion which is found in the city of Nottingham. Over many years, the lion will slowly wear away because of weathering. Describe how different the lion might look in 500 years. What would the lion think about it?!

The lion would, without mantenence, turn into a ovel bazed, blob, of stone with a section sticking out a bit where the head was, it would look very different. This will happen or the stone building would colaps and destroy the lion.

Write your own definition of the three main types of weathering. Use your definitions to play charades with somebody else in your class. Can they guess which type of weathering you are acting out?

Physical weathering: where fisical changes oceer, wind, rain...

Chemical weathering where invisibal changes oceor on a microscopic level, acid rain...

Biological weathering where trees roots or other plants push apart the stone, slowly, as they grow.

From rock to soil 7

1.4 The rock cycle

Here you will learn more about why 'recycling rocks'!

pages 12–13

1 Draw a line to match each definition with its meaning.

Definition	Meaning
Magma	liquid rock at or above the Earth's surface
Erosion	particles of eroded rock or plant and animal debris
Sediment	liquid rock below the Earth's surface
Lava	the process of wearing away rocks

2 Are these statements true or false? Put a tick in the correct box.

	True	False
a. The hard outer part of Earth is cracked into huge slabs, called plates	✓	
b. Below the slabs of rock it is very cold		✓
c. The rock below the slabs is like water	✓	
d. Below the slabs, currents of soft rock flow very quickly		✓
e. Some slabs collide because of these currents of rock	✓	

3 Describe in your own words what the diagram below shows.

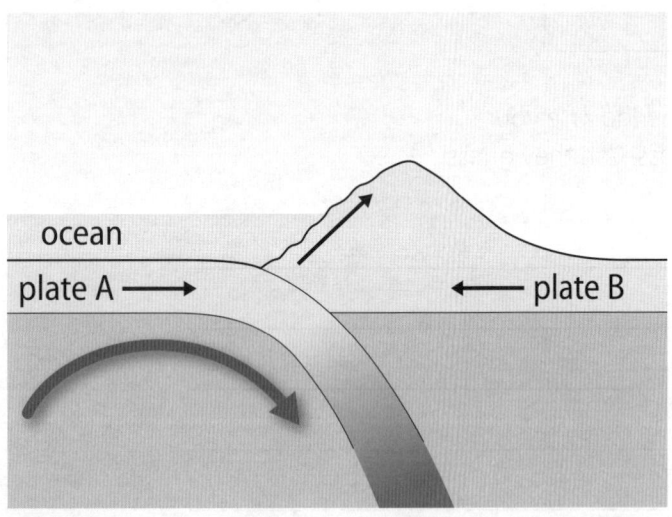

It shows the ocean floor being pulled down under-neeth the land mass, causing it to melt into the mantel.

8 From rock to soil

1.5 The British Isles on their travels

Here you will explore the geological timescale.

1 Printed below are nine events that have happened in geological history. Using the words in the boxes and information from page 15 in **geog.3** to help you, write a paragraph dewscribing how the earth evolved. Remember to use years and the correct names of the geological periods in your answer.

> You will need to put the boxes in the correct order first, so put a number from 1 – 9 at the start of each box!

Dinosaurs become extinct	Mammals and birds thrive	First animals with shells appear
First living cells appear in sea	Giant insects emerge	First birds appear
Warm-blooded reptiles appear	Dinosaurs first appear	Humans appear and spread

From rock to soil

1.6 Rock around the UK

Here you will find out some more about the mountains in the UK.

pages 16–17

1. Using an atlas and other research name the mountains from the descriptions given for each. Also find out the relative height of each mountain, and write your answers in the table below.

Who am I?	Mountain name	Relative height in metres
I am on the west coast of Scotland at the western end of the Grampian mountains. I am close to the town of Fort William and am proud to be the tallest mountain in the British Isles.	Ben Nevis	1344
I am the highest mountain in northern Scotland, north of the Great Glen I am found west-south-west of Inverness. I am very isolated, lying 10km from the nearest road.		
I can be found near the town of Porthmadoc in north Wales. There is a national park named after me. I am the highest point in the British Isles outside of Scotland. I have a railway too!	Snowdon	1085
I am found right in the middle of the Cairngorms National Park and am the second highest mountain in the United Kingdom. They say that I am haunted by a big Grey Man, but I'm not telling!		
Hello! You will find me in in the English county of Cumbria and I am the highest mountain in England! Climb me on a clear day, and you can see Scotland, Wales, Ireland, and the Isle of Man! I am found to the east of Wastwater, one of the famous lakes in the Lake District National Park.		
I am found between Thirlmere and Ullswater, two lakes in the Lake District National Park. I lie north-east of the highest mountain in England and south-east of Keswick.		

2. On the map below the six mountains are numbered 1–6. Write the name of each mountain in the space next to the number.

Number	Mountain name
1	
2	
3	
4	
5	
6	

10 From rock to soil

1.7 Rock and landscapes

Here you will find out some more about limestone landscapes.

pages 18–19

1 How does the acid found in rain affect the limestone?

_____
_____
_____

2 Why is the soil thin in limestone areas?

_____
_____
_____

> As the limestone dissolves, it often leaves gaps where the joints in the limestone are and can form a limestone pavement as shown in the photograph. The gaps are called *grykes* and the blocks are called *clints*.

3 Annotate the photograph to show where the grykes and clints are found. For each, explain how they are formed.

4 Many limestone areas have underground caves. Why do you think caves form underground?

_____
_____
_____
_____

From rock to soil 11

1.8 Soil...and you

Here you will find out why worms are so important.

Hello, I'm Willow the worm!
I have such a busy life, even though I move quite slowly. I have even been called an 'ecosystem engineer'! I can make burrows that are vertical or go sideways, allowing all that lovely oxygen and water to come into the soil.
I don't have a problem choosing what to eat like you humans – if it is rotting, decaying, or organic I will want to have a taste! A lot of my day is spent 'decomposing' – eating and breaking up organic matter such as dead plants and animals so that bacteria and fungi can feed on it and release the lovely nutrients back into the soil. With all this eating it is not surprising that I leave behind castings that are a very valuable type of fertiliser. And that's not all, because as I move I also mix up the soil layers. A famous scientist called Charles Darwin called us 'nature's ploughs' and others have called us 'tiny food processors'!

1 Why do you think worms have been called 'ecosystem engineers'?

  _____
  _____

2 How can worm burrows help plants grow?

  _____
  _____

3 Where do the nutrients come from that go back into the soil after the worm spends its time decomposing?

  _____
  _____

4 Why do you think Darwin called worms 'nature's ploughs'? Do you agree? Why?

  _____
  _____

5 In the space below draw a poster that tells people why worms are so important. Be as creative as you can!

12 From rock to soil

2 Living off Earth's resources

pages 22–23

Since we last visited a strange animal has emerged. It is meant to have intelligence and yet it has allowed its numbers to increase to an extent that it is polluting the water and degrading the soil.

Yes, and it is also destroying all the other animals and cutting down the forests. I wonder what will have happened to Earth when we next visit?

1 How would you explain or defend what humans are doing to the Earth to the two aliens?

_____
_____
_____
_____

2 What do you think will have happened to the Earth when the aliens next visit (in about 10 000 years)?

_____
_____
_____
_____

Living off Earth's resources 13

2.1 Earth's natural resources

Here we look at your own basic needs.

pages 24–25

This Earth we live on provides us with our basic needs (see page 24 in **geog.3**):
Water   Food   Clothing   Shelter   Energy

1 Write down how your own basic needs are met.

Water _____

_____

Food _____

_____

Clothing _____

_____

Shelter _____

_____

Energy _____

_____

2 Explain whether you are satisfied with how your basic needs are met. If not, why not?

_____

_____

_____

_____

_____

_____

14 Living off Earth's resources

2.2 Water around the world

Here we look at the water cycle and consider whether it is a renewable resource.

pages 26–27

1 Write the correct labels in the diagram of the water cycle below.

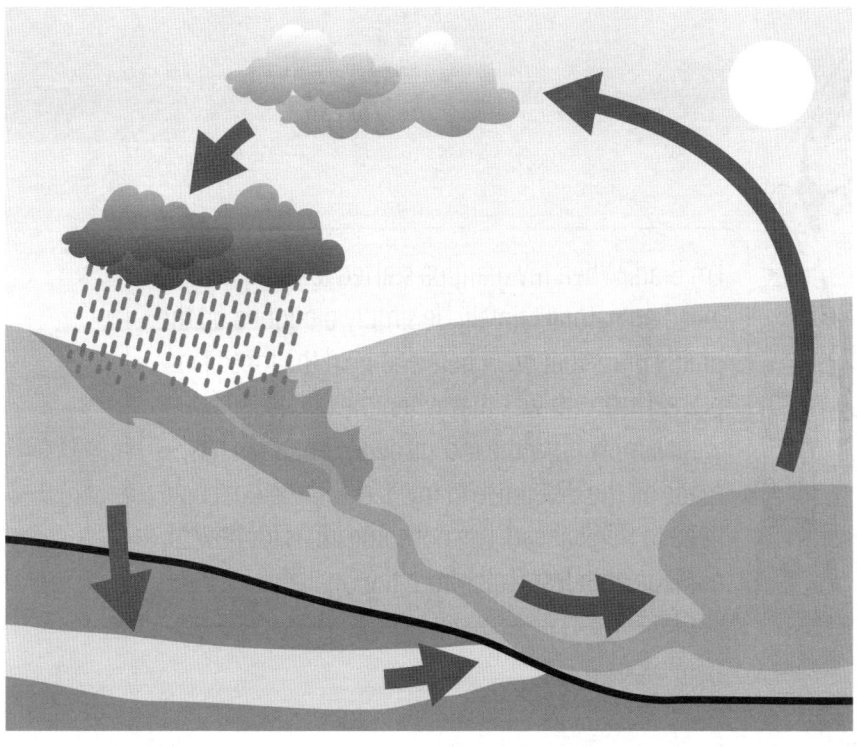

2 In many places we are using fresh water faster than the water cycle can replace it. Can you explain how this can happen?

_____
_____
_____
_____
_____
_____
_____

Living off Earth's resources

2.3 What have they done to the Ogallala?

Here we look at the future for farmers when their underground irrigation water runs out.

I'm Brad. When my grandpa started farming here he relied on natural rainfall. He simply ploughed up the prairie grass that grew here and held the topsoil in place. The result was that when the rain failed the wind simply blew the topsoil away. Irrigation has made all the difference to my dad and me but I now need to think ahead. I've got some ideas for how to manage with less water from the Ogallala.

1. What ideas do you think Brad might come up with to ensure that he can stay living where he is? Check your ideas against suggestions in unit 2.4.

   _____
   _____
   _____
   _____
   _____
   _____

2. Find out where the largest groundwater aquifer in the world is. What makes it less likely to run out of water in the near future compared to the Ogallala?

   _____
   _____
   _____

Living off Earth's resources

2.4 The growing water challenge

Here we look at how the problem of economic water scarcity is being addressed.

geog.3

pages 30–31

WaterAid

WaterAid is an international organization whose mission is to transform the lives of the poorest and most marginalised people by improving access to safe water, sanitation and hygiene.

1 Find out about WaterAid. Write down in your own words what its aims are.

_____

_____

2 Make a list of the different ways in which WaterAid has set about achieving its mission.

_____

_____

_____

_____

_____

_____

_____

3 As explained on page 30 of **geog.3**, it takes six times as much water to produce one kilogram of beef as one kilogram of rice. What are the arguments for taking up the following diets in order to save water?

a Vegetarian (including dairy products and eggs) _____

_____

_____

b Poultry and/or pork _____

_____

_____

c Fish _____

_____

_____

Living off Earth's resources **17**

2.5 Soil...a precious resource

Here we look at the consequences of soil erosion and degradation.

1 Look back at units 2.3 and 2.4 in **geog.3**. Good soil and a sufficient and accessible supply of good quality water are both important for us. Make a list of the comparisons between soil and water in terms of what we are doing to them.

_____
_____
_____
_____

2 There is a good example of soil erosion in unit 2.3 of **geog.3**. Describe what happened to the dustbowl of the USA in the 1930s.

_____
_____
_____
_____

3 Research and give examples of soil degradation in the UK.

_____
_____
_____
_____

18 Living off Earth's resources

2.6 Desertification in the drylands

This is about the possibilities for preventing desertification in the Sahel.

Let's play 'What if?'

Read the flow diagram on page 35 of **geog.3**. It describes the processes that have led to the desertification of the Sahel. If some of the factors were changed then the flow diagram would look quite different. Write down what you think would happen.

1 a If the population wasn't growing then… _____

_____

_____

b If the rains were more reliable then… _____

_____

_____

c If fewer fossil fuels were being burned around the world then… _____

_____

_____

d If more food was produced in the Sahel then… _____

_____

_____

e If fewer people moved into slums in the cities then… _____

_____

_____

2 With changes like the ones you have identified above in mind, rewrite the flow diagram on page 35 of **geog.3** so that it changes from a 'vicious (or bad) cycle' into a 'virtuous (or good) cycle'. What problems do you face in doing this?

_____

_____

_____

_____

_____

_____

_____

Living off Earth's resources   19

2.7 The fight against desertification

pages 36–37

This looks at how social factors can come between people and their efforts to prevent desertification.

I'm not happy with the idea of artificial meat. Cattle mean a lot to us, and not just as a source of food. They are a symbol of a person's importance and an expression of wealth. If our cattle went it would destroy our society.

We have to change in order to survive. Too many cattle, poorly grazed is one of our biggest problems. I am in favour of replacing most of our cattle with crops, carefully cultivated.

1 Which of the two speakers do you agree with? Why?

_____
_____
_____
_____

2 Can you understand the man's point of view? How can rapid change affect a traditional society?

_____
_____
_____
_____

> A traditional society is one where the rules and customs of the past are very important and where change takes place slowly.

20 Living off Earth's resources

2.8 Oil for energy

pages 38–39

This looks at how future generations will judge our reliance on oil.

1 As our use of oil goes up, there are fewer supplies of it left in the ground. What are the arguments for leaving it in the ground for future generations?

2 How do you think students of your age in a hundred years' time will look back on our use of oil?

3 You are a writer in the year 2115. By then all our energy will come from renewable sources. Write an article below titled 'The fossil fuel age'.

Living off Earth's resources   21

2.9 Renewable sources of energy in the UK

This is about the natural sources of energy in the UK.

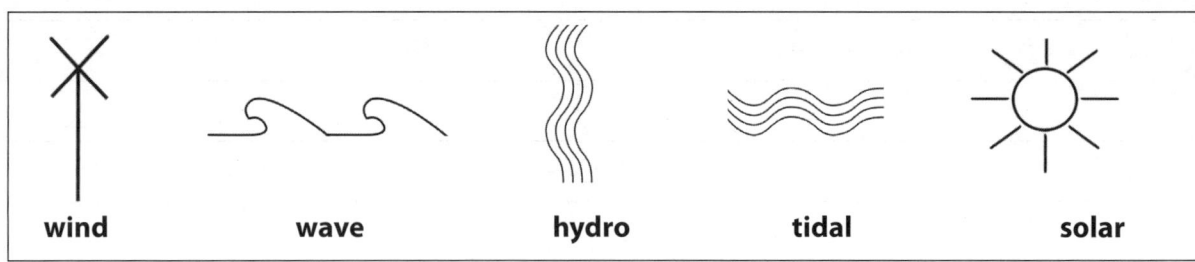

1. Imagine it is 2050. How would this town get its energy? Draw symbols on the town showing what you think should happen.

2. The town has decided to get all of its energy from renewable sources. What problems might there be?

_____
_____
_____
_____
_____

Living off Earth's resources

.10 Solar power around the world

This explains what solar power is, and where it can best be used.

1. Ring the correct word below to complete the sentence.

   Solar power means using energy from COMPOST / RAIN / SUN / WIND.

2. Use the map to give the places in the table a ranking for solar power. Give number 1 to the place best suited for solar power, down to 6 for the place least suited.

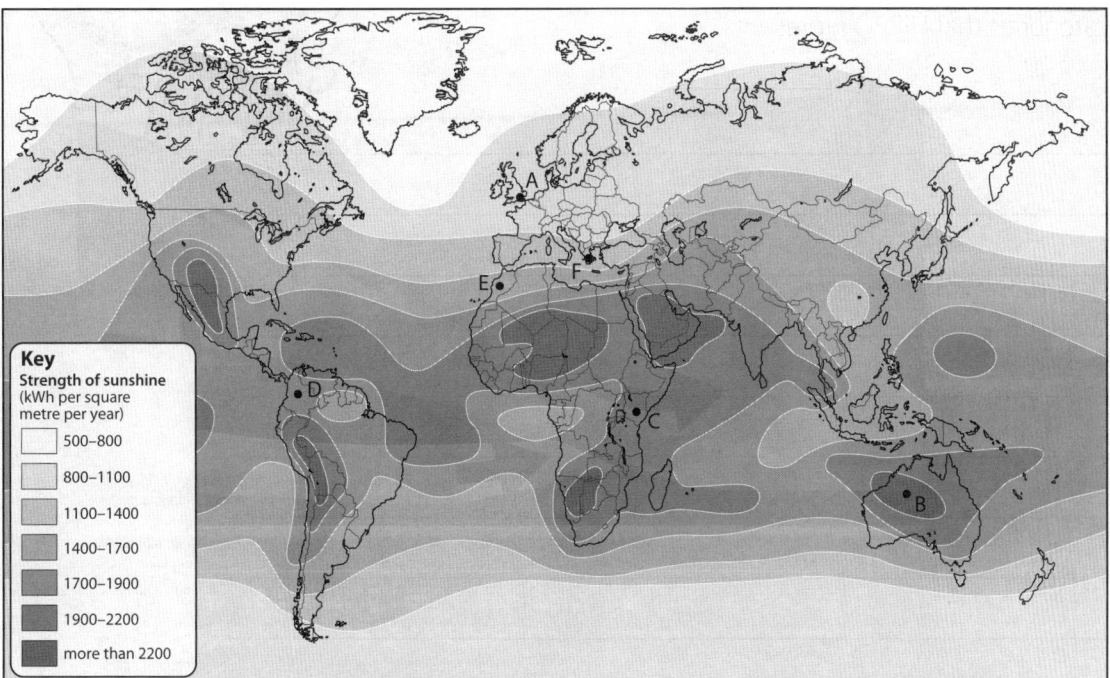

Location on map	Name	Ranking
A	Britain	
B	Australia	
C	Kenya	
D	Colombia	
E	Morocco	
F	Greece	

Key
Strength of sunshine (kWh per square metre per year)
- 500–800
- 800–1100
- 1100–1400
- 1400–1700
- 1700–1900
- 1900–2200
- more than 2200

Solar power is useful because the PV cells can convert sunlight into electrical energy on a stand-alone system. This means they don't need to be connected to a national grid and can be sited anywhere (providing there is enough sunlight!).

3. Complete the two speech bubbles for Jomo, a Kenyan schoolboy living in an isolated small village. What does he think about the possibilities of solar power?

   My country is sunny all year round, so …

   My school is miles from anywhere, but …

Living off Earth's resources 23

2.11 But what about other species?

Here we consider the threats from human activity to biodiversity.

The word that is used to express the number and variety of animal and plant species is 'biodiversity'. One term that is used to express the greatest threats to biodiversity is **HIPPO**, standing for **H**abitat destruction, **I**nvasive species, **P**ollution, human over-**P**opulation, and **O**ver-harvesting.

1. Refer to pages 44–45 in **geog.3** and research on the internet to give examples of each of the categories that HIPPO represents.

Habitat destruction _____
_____
_____
_____

Invasive species _____
_____
_____
_____

Pollution _____
_____
_____
_____

human over-**P**opulation _____
_____
_____
_____

Over-harvesting _____
_____
_____
_____

Living off Earth's resources

3 Earning a living

pages 46–47

Your own job survey

This chapter will look into the way in which the employment structure of the UK has changed in recent times.

1. Find out for yourself how the jobs in your family or among other older people you know have changed. Ask your parents, guardians or any older person you know what their grandparents (4th generation) did for a living; then what their parents (3rd generation) did for a living. Then make a note of what your parents or the generation above you (2nd generation) did or do for a living. Then write down what you (1st generation) would like to do for a living, and why.

4th generation _____
_____
_____

3rd generation _____
_____
_____

2nd generation _____
_____
_____

1st generation _____
_____
_____

2. Describe the changes in the kinds of work that members of your family or older people you know have undertaken over the past 4 generations.

_____
_____
_____
_____
_____

Earning a living 25

3.1 The UK at work

This is about the kind of work people in the UK do for a living.

1 What is an *employment sector*?
   _____

2 **a** Cross out the wrong word in each sentence.

   The secondary/primary sector is when you gather materials from the earth.

   The secondary/quaternary sector is when you do hi-tech research.

   The primary/tertiary sector is when you provide a service for people.

   The tertiary/secondary sector is when you turn materials into things to sell.

   b Now give two example of jobs in each sector.

   Primary:
   _____

   Secondary:
   _____

   Tertiary:
   _____

   Quaternary:
   _____

3 In the UK, about 26 million people work for a living. This pie chart shows the kind of work we do in the UK.

   a Shade in the boxes in the key, each a different colour.

   b Now shade in the different sections of the pie chart to show the kind of work we do.

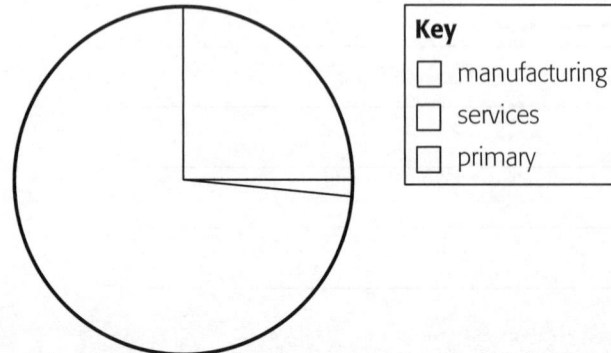

26 Earning a living

3.2 So where are the jobs?

This is about the factors that influence where the best-paying jobs are – and some of the reasons why.

1 What helps to make an area wealthy? Cross out the things that don't help, so that you're left with the things that do.

Things that help make a place wealthy

- good farmland
- oil (or other valuable mineral)
- companies offering poorly-paid jobs
- few transport links
- beautiful countryside
- interesting history
- land that is not good for farming
- little industry
- museums and other tourist attractions
- flourishing industry
- no tourist attractions
- plenty of companies offering highly-skilled and highly-paid employment
- easy access (having good road links for example)

2 This is Anya. She works at a large museum which attracts lots of tourists. It was set up a few years ago by a grant from the government.

Fill in the speech bubble to say how the museum has affected Anya and the local area.

Three years ago, I had no job and very little money. It was really tough. I thought about moving away because the area felt so run down. It was
_____
_____

Now things are different. What happened was
_____
_____
_____

I feel _____
_____

The local area has changed too …
_____
_____
_____
_____
_____

Earning a living 27

3.3 The UK's changing employment structure

Here we consider what changes in our employment structure lie ahead.

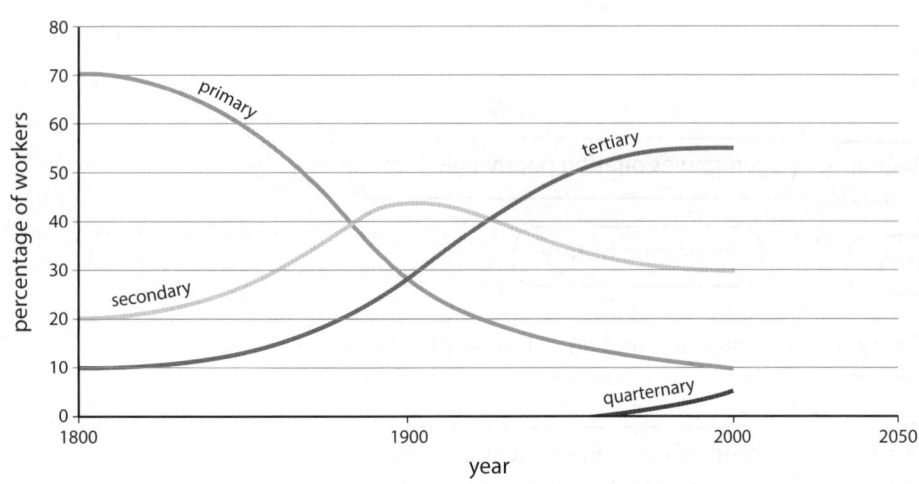

Look at the graph, which appeared in **geog.3**. Extend the lines according to how you think the graph might look in 2050. Consider the following:
- Our farmers still produce 60% of the food we eat.
- Manufacturing has started to return to the UK.
- Automation in the service sector is increasing.

Don't forget that the four lines have to add up to 100%!

1 Although our agricultural sector is still an important part of the economy, it represents a very small percentage of the workforce. Why is this?

    _____
    _____

2 Factory workers in less-developed countries are becoming more prosperous. How might this affect manufacturing in the UK?

    _____
    _____

3 If manufacturing begins to return to the UK, will it provide the same number of jobs as before? If not, why not?

    _____
    _____

4 The UK leads the world in the creation and design of computer games. Why do you think that this activity can be described as part of the quaternary sector?

    _____
    _____

Earning a living

3.4 Change in and around Doncaster

Here we look at the different sorts of jobs that Doncaster can offer.

pages 54–55

I used to be a coalminer. I've been unemployed for 10 years. The sort of job I want is…

I want to start up a stall or small retail outlet selling my home made cakes and bread as well as locally sourced cheese. What I need is…

I've just left college with a qualification in software development. The sort of job I want is…

1 All three of the people above live in Doncaster. Complete their statements.

2 Which of the three is the most likely to leave Doncaster in search of work? Why?

_____

_____

3 Research the tourist attractions in and around Doncaster. Given its long history and the many local attractions, what do you think could be done to boost Doncaster's tourist industry?

_____

_____

_____

_____

_____

Earning a living

3.5 Employment structure in other countries

Here we look at the changes in the employment structure of other countries.

1 Look at the pie graphs for the UK, China and Ethiopia on page 56 of **geog.3** as well as the flow chart on page 57 showing the usual way in which the employment structure of a country changes over time.

What would you expect the employment structure of Ethiopia to look like by 2050? Consider all the factors that have been affecting the employment structure in the UK in the past. Draw it onto the pie chart below. Draw a key next to it.

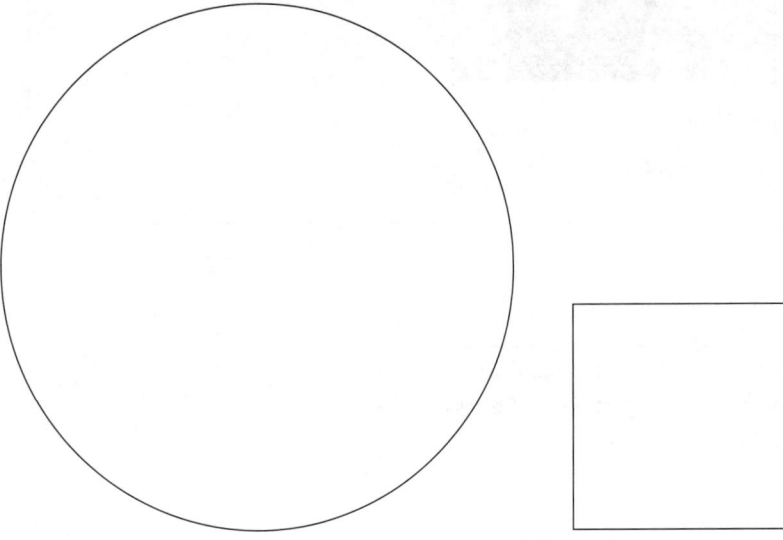

2 Can you explain what led you to your decision?

_____
_____
_____

3 Is your pie graph for Ethiopia 2050 different from that of China today? If so, why?

_____
_____
_____
_____

30   Earning a living

3.6 Where did the UK's factory jobs go?

This deals with the sort of manufacturing that the UK is good at.

> I own a factory making high quality shoes. Our craftsmen are among the best in the world. Our shoes may cost several times more than foreign made shoes but they will last you a lifetime. You get what you pay for.

1 What are the problems with the businessman's argument?

   _____
   _____

2 What are the arguments in favour of buying quality goods?

   _____
   _____

> We have a long tradition of film making and of high quality drama schools in this country. So British made movies and British actors are very successful.

3 Write down any British films, actors or directors that have been a worldwide success.

   _____
   _____

> I run a printing company. We have invested in the latest technology and now offer the same quality as overseas printers. We are a bit more expensive but we can deliver to our customers a lot quicker than magazines or books printed in China.

4 Draw up a list of other products where speed of delivery is important.

   _____
   _____

Earning a living **31**

3.7 The clothing industry in Bangladesh

pages 60–61

This is about how some of our clothes are made by exploiting people in poorer countries, like Bangladesh.

1 Write a definition for each of these terms:

   a *Exploit*: to _____

   b *Sweatshop*: a place where _____

2 Look at this flow diagram, which shows how a garment is produced and sold.

   Designer → Company executive → Factory owner → Workers → Shoppers

   a Colour in red those boxes that will be in a developing country.

   b Colour in blue those boxes that will be in a developed country.

   c Who is the exploiter? _____

   d Who is being exploited? _____

   e Which of the people in the chain has the most power? Explain your answer.

   _____
   _____

   f Suggest how you might help to improve conditions for the workers.

   _____
   _____

3 a True or False? Write T or F beside each of the following statements.

   • Workers like Munna are well paid. ☐
   • Workers like Munna often work long hours. ☐
   • Most sweatshops are in developed countries. ☐
   • Companies that make clothes look for factories in developing countries because wages there are lower. ☐
   • If a factory pays its workers more, it makes a bigger profit. ☐
   • If a factory in a developing country has no orders, the workers are likely to be sacked. ☐
   • If an item of clothing has a designer label, it means the person who made it is paid more. ☐
   • An item of clothing made in the UK is likely to cost less than if it was made in a developing country. ☐

   b Rewrite one of the statements you said was false, so that it becomes true.

   _____

Earning a living

3.8 Working to bring you a mobile

This is about the arguments for and against globalisation.

1. Complete the following statements, using the words from the box. (You may need to use some words more than once.)

   - Multinationals are more powerful than the _____ of many countries.
   - Multinationals are not elected, and their decisions are driven by _____
   - Multinationals exploit _____ as a source of cheap labour.
   - Multinationals create unemployment in _____
   - The factories of some Multinationals pollute the _____
   - Most Multinationals have their HQ in _____ , so their profits do not benefit _____
   - It is hard for some _____ to control the actions of Multinationals.

   > governments
   > profit
   > developing countries
   > developed countries
   > environment

2. **a** Look at the table. Decide which arguments are For and which Against globalisation. Circle your chosen answer in red.

   b Then decide which arguments can be described as Social, Economic, or Environmental. Circle your answer in blue. (You may want to circle more than one possible answer.)

Argument	For or against?	Social (S), economic (Ec), and/or environmental (En)?
Globalisation breaks down barriers between countries.	For / Against	S / Ec / En
Globalsation causes unemployment in some developed countries.	For / Against	S / Ec / En
When a multinational opens a factory in a developing country, it helps that country to develop.	For / Against	S / Ec / En
The activities of some multinationals can pollute an area.	For / Against	S / Ec / En
Multinationals look for the cheapest source of labour.	For / Against	S / Ec / En
Globalisation can change the culture of a developing country.	For / Against	S / Ec / En
The wages earned by people in developing countries help their country to develop.	For / Against	S / Ec / En
Many developing countries do not have adequate laws to make sure the water and air are kept clean.	For / Against	S / Ec / En
Globalisation gives people a wide choice over what they can buy.	For / Against	S / Ec / En
Multinationals help developing countries to exploit their resources.	For / Against	S / Ec / En

3. Referring to the arguments in question 2, select one that is for globalisation, and one that is against it. For each one, write a short paragraph to support that argument.

For: _____

_____

_____

_____

Against: _____

_____

_____

_____

Earning a living

4 International development

pages 64–65

1 Look at the photo on page 64 of **geog.3**. What do you think is happening?

_____

2 Why do you think it has been chosen to introduce a chapter on international development?

_____

_____

3 Would you describe the people in the photo as poor? Why, or why not?

_____

_____

_____

_____

4 Do you think they are poor compared with poor people in the UK? Why, or why not?

_____

_____

_____

_____

_____

34 International development

4.1 Rich world, poor world

This is about how unequal our world is.

1 The shaded areas in the pie graphs below show the following:

   a) the 77% of people around the world who live on less than $10 a day;

   b) the 24% of people who have no electricity;

   c) the 8% of people who never get enough to eat, ever – who are starving;

   d) the 1 in 5 people aged over 15 who can't read or write.

Match the numbers against the pies to the letters above.

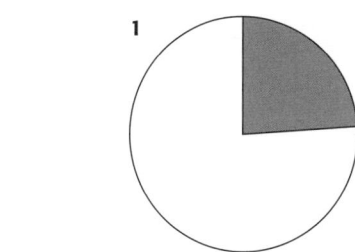
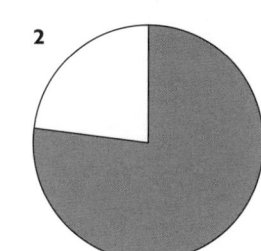

1 = _____   2 = _____

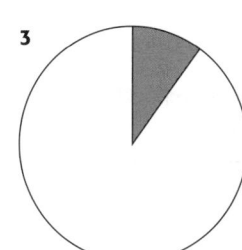
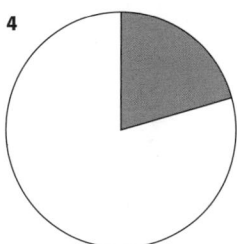

3 = _____   4 = _____

2 Here some statistics about the countries that Hannah, Joe, Julien and Nisha live in. They are the USA, Bolivia, Ghana and Nepal. Match the statistics to the country. [Note that 'adult illiteracy' means the percentage of people over 15 who cannot read or write.]

Country 1
GDP = $1500
Adult illiteracy = 42.1%
Infant mortality = 51/1000 live births
Life expectancy = 60
Size clue: same size as the UK

Country 2
GDP = $1100
Adult illiteracy = 51.4%
Infant mortality = 47/1000 live births
Life expectancy = 65.5
Size clue: twice the size of Scotland

Country 3
GDP = $4500
Adult illiteracy = 13.3%
Infant mortality = 44.5/1000 live births
Life expectancy = 67
Size clue: four times the size of the UK

Country 4
GDP = $44 000
Adult illiteracy = 1%
Infant mortality = 6.3/1000 live births
Life expectancy = 78
Size clue: slightly larger than China

Country 1 = _____   Country 2 = _____   Country 3 = _____   Country 4 = _____

International development

4.2 So what is development?

This is about different aspects of development.

pages 68–69

1. Complete the spider diagram below, using the words and statements from the box. (You will need to add more 'legs' to the diagram.)

☺ education for everyone	☺ more health care for everyone	☺ justice
☺ lower pollution	☺ living longer	☺ more money for the country
☺ equality for women	☺ sustainability	☺ fewer children dying
☺ more jobs		

2. Then add some more ideas of your own.

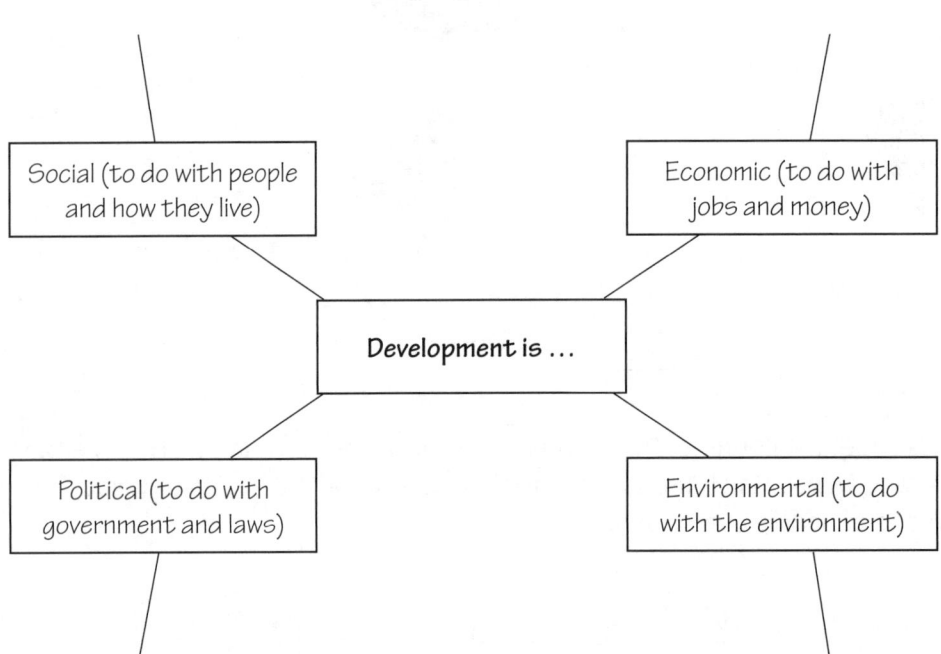

36 International development

4.3 Measuring and mapping development

This is about identifying developed and developing countries around the world.

geog.3
pages 70–71

1 Finish off these sentences:

Richer countries are called developed. That means … _____

Poorer ones are called developing. That means … _____

2 If you landed in a strange country and didn't know where you were, how could you tell if it was developed? Think of at least five ways.

_____

_____

_____

_____

_____

3 The names of 15 countries are hidden in this wordsearch. Some are developed and some are developing.

You need two colours. Use one colour to mark the names of the developed countries as you find them in the wordsearch. Use the other colour to mark the names of the developing countries. The names of the countries you're looking for are:

Australia
Brazil
Canada
Egypt
Ghana
India
Japan
Kenya
New Zealand
Peru
Somalia
Sweden
United Kingdom
USA
Zimbabwe

h	o	z	y	a	b	n	e	d	e	w	s	l	a	x
m	a	r	t	i	r	j	a	p	a	n	t	n	n	p
e	o	b	q	d	a	m	c	r	w	v	a	y	j	b
q	g	d	s	n	z	y	y	m	c	h	d	b	t	l
k	j	y	g	i	i	s	z	a	g	v	n	a	g	e
w	f	s	p	n	l	y	n	n	a	u	a	r	y	o
w	h	z	o	t	i	a	d	i	g	z	l	n	b	k
a	z	w	n	m	d	k	l	m	r	x	a	f	v	k
u	u	y	u	a	a	a	d	a	r	g	e	k	n	m
w	s	f	q	u	r	l	b	e	y	a	z	p	i	h
y	j	n	s	t	r	h	i	g	t	n	w	i	w	c
d	d	a	s	i	e	p	y	a	r	i	e	g	p	p
r	p	u	z	i	m	b	a	b	w	e	n	k	e	g
h	a	s	q	c	b	o	q	m	y	b	w	u	r	a
d	l	b	q	v	y	b	h	g	q	i	u	c	u	h

International development **37**

4.4 Malawi: a developing country

Here we look at Sephora's life and at some of the problems that Malawi faces.

pages 72–73

1 Imagine you are Sephora. In your own words, describe what you do during the day.

At 6.15 am I ... _____

_____

At 7 am I ... _____

_____

At 1 pm I ... _____

_____

At 6 pm I ... _____

_____

At 7 pm I ... _____

_____

2 Explain what your hopes are for the future. Are they likely to happen? If not, why not?

_____

_____

_____

3 Malawi depends more and more on tobacco sales for export earnings. Why might this be a problem in the future?

_____

_____

_____

International development

4.5 Singapore: a developed country

Here we look at aspects of life in Singapore.

1 Read the account of Cheng's day in **geog.3**.

   a What are the good things about Cheng's life?

   _____
   _____
   _____

   b What things about Cheng's life do you not envy?

   _____
   _____
   _____

2 Singapore has become one of the wealthiest countries in the world. But it has lost about 90% of its natural forests since 1980. And there are problems with air and water pollution. Has this been a price worth paying, in your view?

   _____
   _____
   _____

3 Two out of five people in Singapore is a foreign worker. They have helped Singapore to succeed. But there is no minimum wage or social safety net. Is this a price worth paying, in your view?

   _____
   _____
   _____

4 Who would you rather be, Cheng or Sephora? Why?

   _____
   _____
   _____

International development

4.6 How did the development gap grow? – part 1

This is about the reasons for the development gap.

1. The paragraphs below are all about why some countries are poorer than others. The words in brackets are all jumbled up though! You need to unscramble them and write them on the lines.

_____

Many poorer countries were once (cilnoodes) _____ by European countries. The Europeans took raw (atameirls) _____ and turned them into finished (gsdoo) _____. They sold these goods back to the poorer country! When the colonisers left, the countries had little (iustrnyd) _____, people didn't have much (edcaution) _____ or many (ssklli) _____.

_____

Some poorer countries have difficult (matescli) _____ so they can't grow (fdoo) _____.

_____

A country has a better chance of developing if it is (ecuesre) _____, but some poorer countries have (sraw) _____. They also have (ropctur) _____ leaders who make themselves rich while their people live in (rvoypet) _____.

---

2. The reasons above can be divided into three groups. Match the titles of the groups with their meanings by drawing linking lines.

historical reasons	reasons that are about natural resources, rainfall, temperature, soils and landscapes
social and political reasons	reasons that are about what happened in the past, like colonisation
geographical reasons	reasons that are about politics and money

3. In the space above each paragraph in the box, you are going to write its title. Use the group titles from question **2**.

International development

4.7 How did the development gap grow? – part 2

This is about the factors that keep the development gap wide.

geog.3
pages 78–79

Here is a list of the Heavily Indebted Poor Countries (HIPCs) that have qualified for and received financial help.

[Note. To qualify for HIPC status a country has to prove that it cannot pay off its debt even after it has received all normal debt assistance.]

| Benin   Guinea   Guinea-Bissau   Honduras   Madagascar   Malawi   Mali   Mauretania   Mozambique Nicaragua   Bolivia   Burkina Faso   Cameroon   Chad   Democratic Republic of Congo   Ethiopia   Gambia Ghana   Niger   Rwanda   Sao Tome and Principe   Sierra Leone   Senegal   Tanzania   Uganda   Zambia |

Colour in the HIPC countries in Africa on the map above. Then cross them off the list above.

1   Which countries on the list are **not** in Africa?

_____

_____

_____

2   Can you explain why some African countries like South Africa and Egypt are not on the list?

_____

_____

_____

International development   41

4.8 Escaping from poverty

This is about the different kinds of migrants.

geog.3 pages 80–81

> My home town is under the control of drug barons. I want a better life for my children.

> We belong to a different religion from the people attacking us. If they catch us we will have to convert to their religion or die.

> The bombs started falling and our home was destroyed. We were lucky to escape. Now we have no home. We will be killed if we return.

> We were starving in our village. The rains had failed and there is no work in our cities. We want to come to Europe for a new life.

1 Some of the people shown could be called refugees and some migrants. Is it possible to make a distinction between them? What are your views?

_____
_____
_____
_____
_____

International development

4.9 Putting an end to poverty

Trade or aid? This looks at the arguments.

geog.3
pages 82–83

1 The arguments in favour of aid or trade to help developing countries has been going on for a long time. Read the arguments for and against below and then give your opinions.

Arguments in favour of trade
- **Trade** makes a developing country more independent of the aid-giving countries. Aid budgets can always be cut.
- **Trade** helps developing countries to maintain their dignity Aid can be seen as a form of charity.
- **Trade** establishes a strong impression in the international market.
- **Trade** improves the economic performance of a country while aid money can be misused. Aid can lead to corruption.

Arguments in favour of aid
- **Aid** can go directly to where it is needed, while trade can distribute resources inefficiently. The benefit of trade is mostly confined to an elite group of people within the country.
- **Aid** is not always provided in the form of money and is sometimes provided through expert advisors. On the other hand, trade needs a good infrastructure of the country to prosper. It is very difficult for the developing countries to maintain a good infrastructure.
- **Aid** allows for money in a given country to be allocated well against need.
- Exposing fragile developing economies to free **trade** is very risky.
- **Trade** requires investment first.
- **Trade** does not necessarily mean **Fair trade**

Aid or trade? _____

_____

_____

_____

_____

_____

_____

_____

_____

International development   43

5 Our restless planet

Until about 200 million years ago there was one great super continent called Pangea, but then it split up into two continents, Laurasia and Gondwanaland. Then about 180 million years ago Gondwanaland and Laurasia began to split up and eventually today's continents were formed as a result of the movement of the Earth's plates.

1. Look at the map of the world today at the top of the page. Try to identify today's continents on the map of Laurasia and Gondwanaland below which shows the world when the two continents began to split from Pangea. On the map below, write down the names of today's seven continents and one sub-continent.

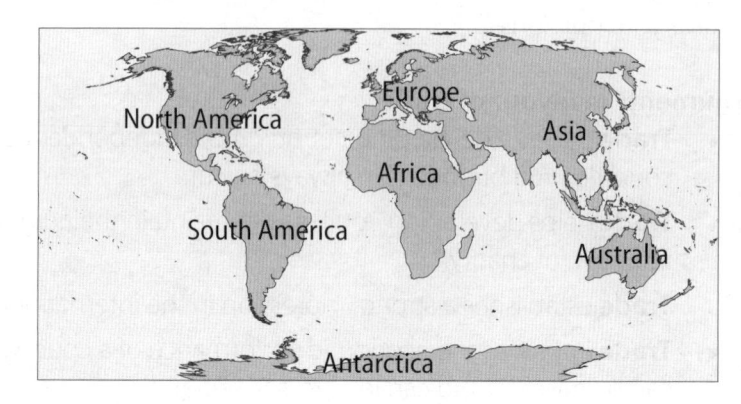

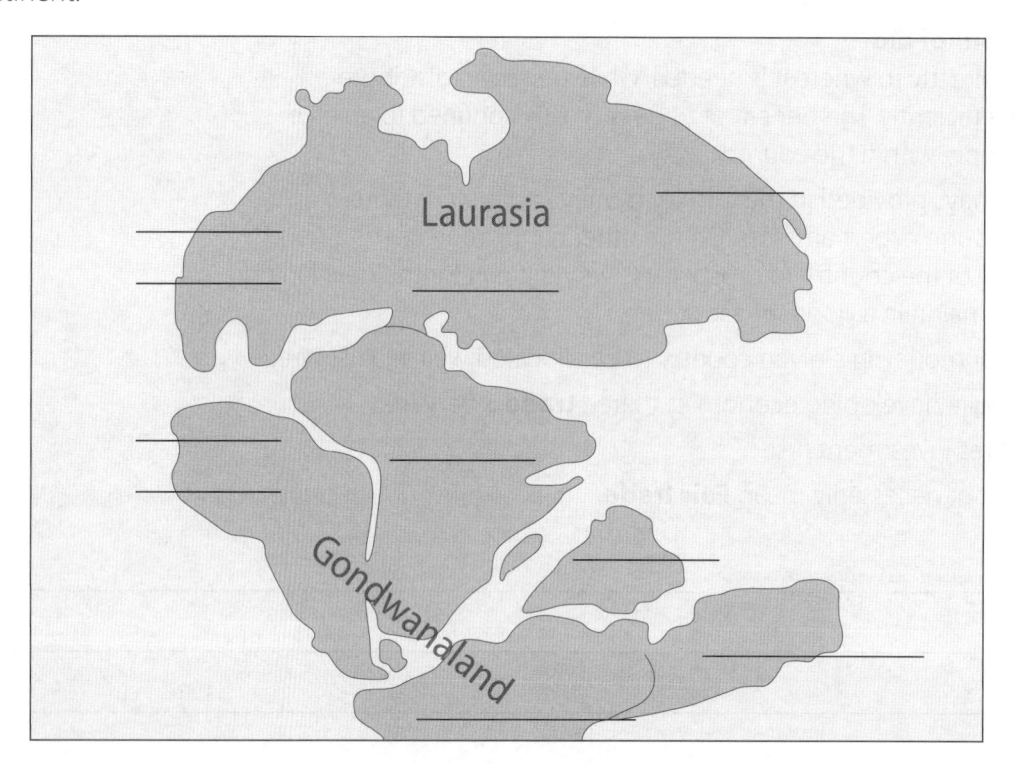

2. What sort of evidence have scientists uncovered to show that the earth's continents were once joined together? Look for answers on the internet.

_____
_____
_____
_____
_____

44 Our restless planet

5.1 A slice through Earth

This is about the three layers that make up the Earth.

1 This diagram shows the layers that make up the Earth.

  a Choose the words from the box and label them correctly on the diagram.

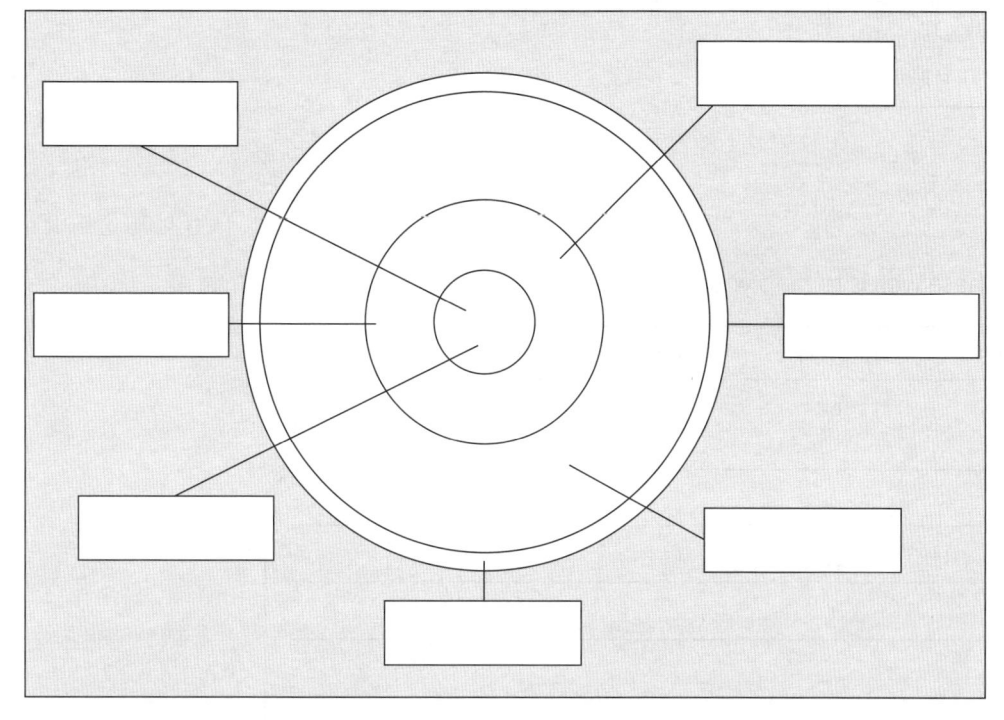

| solid | mantle | liquid | hard rock | crust | inner core | outer core |

  b Now colour the inner core yellow, the outer core orange, the mantle brown and the crust black.

Now try these…

2 What is the lithosphere composed of? _____

_____

3 a What is the radius of the Earth? _____

  b How can you use this figure to work out the circumference of the Earth?
     (Clue: think **pi**)

_____

_____

_____

  c What is the circumference of the Earth? _____

4 There are two types of crust, continental and oceanic. What are the differences between them?

_____

_____

Our restless planet

5.2 Our cracked Earth

This is about where the Earth's plates are – and their link with earthquakes and volcanoes.

Why do earthquakes and volcanoes happen mostly in the same place?

1 Write a reply to this question. Use these words to help you.

| plates | crust | margins | moving | convection |

Well, it's because . . .
_____
_____
_____
_____
_____
_____
_____

2 Why don't earthquakes and volcanoes happen in some places?
_____
_____

3 Why are the Himalayas increasing in height?
_____
_____

4 Why are volcanoes frequent in Iceland?
_____
_____

5 Why are there no major earthquakes in Britain?
_____
_____

46 Our restless planet

5.3 A closer look at plate movements

This is about how the Earth's plates are moving – and how their movements produce earthquakes, volcanoes, and even mountains!

geog.3
pages 90–91

1 These pictures show the different kinds of plate margins.

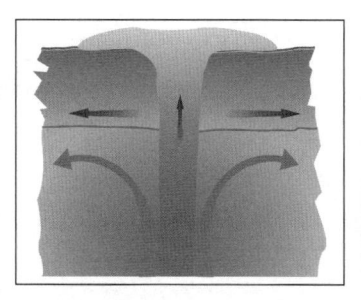

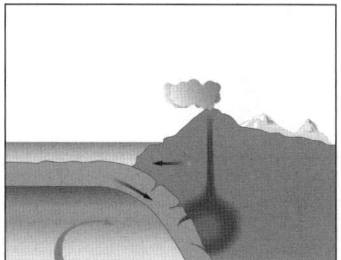

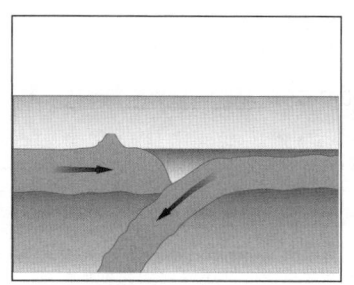

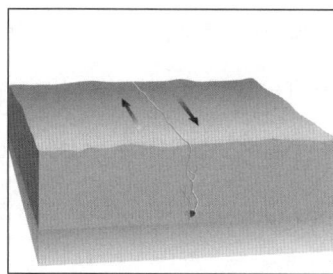

_____   _____   _____   _____
_____   _____   _____   _____
_____   _____   _____   _____
_____   _____   _____   _____

- **a** Label each diagram. Choose from:
  - plates are moving apart
  - plates are sliding past each other
  - one oceanic plate is going under a continental one
  - two continental plates pushing into each other

- **b** Draw a red star on the diagrams where you would expect earthquakes to happen.

- **c** Label any volcanoes you would expect.

- **d** Label the fold mountains.

- **e** Label the new crust that's being formed.

2 Which diagram do you think shows a **constructive** (building) margin? Why?

_____
_____
_____

3 Which diagram do you think shows a **destructive** (destroying) margin? Why?

_____
_____
_____

Our restless planet   **47**

5.4 Earthquakes

This is about what earthquakes are, and how they are measured, and what damage they do.

geog.3
pages 92–93

Answer these questions to find the words that are hidden in the wordsearch.

1 Waves that are made by earthquakes _____
2 Small earthquakes after the main one _____
3 The point inside the crust where the earthquake started _____
4 The point on the surface right above where the earthquake started _____
5 Amount of energy that an earthquake gives out _____
6 A machine that measures the magnitude of the earthquake _____
7 The scale that tells us how strong an earthquake is _____
8 A tidal wave caused by earthquakes _____
9 What an earthquake makes the ground do _____
10 If gas pipes fracture there might be _____
11 Now find these words in the wordsearch!

r	v	e	e	e	o	u	t	z	w	h	p	u	w	c
w	e	f	m	f	a	c	s	u	s	a	x	f	g	j
w	p	t	o	v	x	p	u	m	y	e	m	j	w	a
v	v	c	e	h	s	c	n	i	d	g	r	q	p	e
r	u	z	b	m	f	f	a	m	s	d	e	i	d	x
s	i	b	a	b	o	r	m	k	m	r	r	u	f	h
q	v	c	t	c	g	m	i	y	p	y	t	d	n	b
v	h	u	h	f	x	f	s	w	u	i	n	b	e	m
o	d	a	y	t	d	q	c	i	n	o	e	s	e	n
e	k	a	h	s	e	v	s	g	e	b	c	k	t	m
h	a	e	t	y	o	r	a	q	p	s	i	m	l	r
t	p	s	e	i	s	m	i	c	p	w	p	k	f	e
s	k	c	o	h	s	r	e	t	f	a	e	c	x	e
d	x	y	f	x	c	x	v	n	d	p	s	n	k	u
b	u	z	p	p	v	h	o	h	c	l	j	y	y	r

48   Our restless planet

5.5 An earthquake in Southwest China

This is about the damage caused in the Sichuan earthquake of 2008.

The earthquake factfile

date	Monday 12 May 2008
time	2.28 pm
magnitude	7.9 on the Richter scale
epicentre	in mountains in Sichuan province, southwest China
damage	over 87 000 people killed over 370 000 people injured, and over 5 million people left homeless in Sichuan province
financial cost	nearly £120 billion

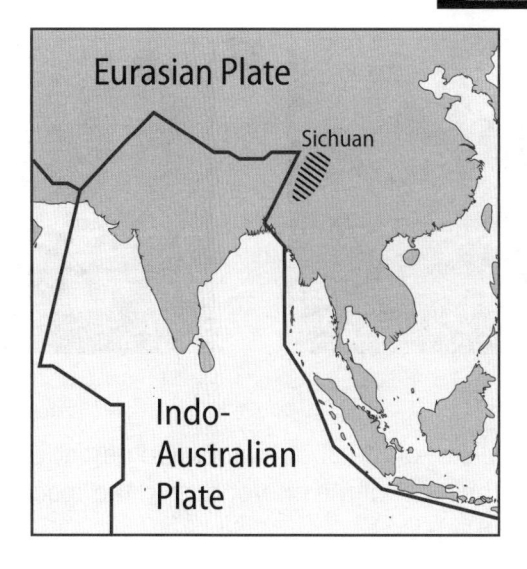

1 Using the information from the map and the Factfile, add words to the speech bubble to complete what the two people are saying.

This is what caused the earthquake.

The damage was terrible.

2 Look at the table below. Put a tick in the column to show if what happened could have been stopped or not.

Event	Could not be stopped	Could be stopped
1 The two plates are colliding and causing a lot of strain		
2 On 12 May the strain got too much		
3 At 2.28 in the afternoon the ground shook		
4 Buildings in Beichuan Middle School collapse		
5 Rock slipped as much as 12 metres along the fault		
6 Parents blamed local officials for erecting poorly built schools		
7 Many people helped, including the army		
8 Students and teachers were crushed to death		
9 Over 87 000 people were killed		

Our restless planet

5.6 Tsunami!

This is about the damage tsunamis do to the environment, the economy and people.

pages 96–97

A **B** **C** **D**

1 Choose one of the photographs and describe the damage that you can see.
Write the letter of the photograph in the space.
Photograph [ ]

_____
_____
_____
_____

2 Complete the table below to describe the damage caused to the environment, the economy and people.

	Natural (environment)	Economic (business/money)	Social (people)
Photograph A			
Photograph B			
Photograph C			
Photograph D			

50 Our restless planet

5.7 Volcanoes

This is about what volcanoes are, and the damage an eruption can do.

Volcanoes happen on the edges of plates, where one plate goes under another. Sometimes the plate suddenly starts moving and you get a new volcano where there wasn't one before.

This is what happened in Mexico …

Draw a picture for each of the boxes in this cartoon strip.

1 It was 1943. In a flat maize (corn on the cob) field in Mexico…

2 … smoke and ash were seen coming from the ground.

3 The ground cracked and there was a terrible smell like rotten eggs.

4 By the next morning the cone of ash was as tall as a house.

5 Over the next year the cone built up with layers of ash and lava to make a new volcano. It was named after the nearest village – Paricutin.

6 The mountain erupted for 9 years! By the end it had covered 10 square miles in lava and killed over 1000 people.

7 The lava and ash caused damage during the eruption but left the soil fertile (good and rich) so now lots of crops can be grown and livestock (farm animals) graze the land.

8 Now Paricutin is nearly 400 metres high

Our restless planet 51

5.8 Iceland: a country made by volcanoes

This is about Iceland; a unique volcanic country.

1 Here is a list islands or island groups that occur along the Mid-Atlantic Ridge. Using an atlas, find out where they are and mark and label them on the map below.

Tristan da Cunha   St Helena   the Azores   Gough Island
Ascension   St Paul's Rocks

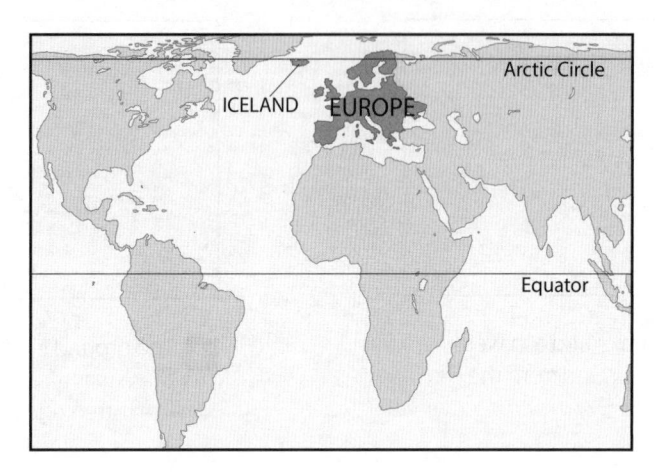

2 In Iceland there is a place called Geyser, after which all other geysers are named! What is a geyser?

_____
_____

3 On 15 November 1963 there was an underwater eruption just off the south coast of Iceland and a new island was formed, Surtsey. Find out more about Surtsey. Why would a brand new island be of special interest to scientists, especially biologists?

_____
_____
_____
_____
_____

Our restless planet

5.9 Why live in a danger zone?

Here we consider issues around living in an earthquake zone.

geog.3
pages 102–103

1. Since 1836 there have been 5 major earthquakes in the San Francisco area, plus 15 smaller but damaging earthquakes. The probability of a magnitude 7 earthquake in the next 30 years is about 75 per cent. You have been offered an exciting long-term job in San Francisco. Give the arguments for and against accepting the job.

   For _____
   _____

   Against _____
   _____

   What would **you** decide? Why? _____
   _____

2. Geothermal energy is renewable and continuous. Ninety per cent of Iceland's energy is produced this way. Why is it more difficult to produce geothermal energy in the UK?

   _____
   _____

3. In 2014 there were major earthquakes in Chile and Haiti. Earthquakes occur often in Chile while they are a lot less common in Haiti, one of the poorest countries in the world.

   The Chile earthquake recorded 8.2 on the Richter scale and there was a loss of life of 6 people. The Haiti earthquake recorded 7.0 on the Richter scale and there was a loss of life of about 220,000.

   Can you account for the difference in the death toll between the two earthquakes?

   _____
   _____
   _____
   _____
   _____
   _____

Our restless planet 53

6 Russia

1 Russia is a huge country; by area, it is the largest country on earth. In fact, it is so big that it is the largest country in two continents, Asia and Europe! The photographs on page 104 of **geog.3** each show different aspects of Russia.

Choose the one photograph that you think best represents Russia. Make a sketch of it in the space below and add labels explaining why you chose it.

6.1 Meet Russia

Here you will explain a little more about Russia.

1. The overview shown on page 107 in **geog.3** gives nine facts about Russia. Imagine that you are a visitor to Russia. Write a postcard home explaining what you expect your visit to Russia to be like.

> Use your imagination, as well as facts about the country!

A postcard from Russia

6.2 A little history

Here you will explore more about Russia's past.

pages 108–109

1. Over any years Russia has undergone great change. Using the information on pages 108–109 in **geog.3** to help you, choose the three most significant events that you think have helped shape modern Russia.

   Give reasons for your choice of each event.

I think that the most significant event in Russia's history is …

I think this is the most significant because…

What events helped shape Russia?

I think that the second most significant event in Russia's history is …

I think this because…

I think that the third most significant event is…

I think this because …

Russia

6.3 Russia's main physical features

Here you will find out more about Russia's 'Mother Volga'.

The Volga River is Europe's longest river, over 2200 miles long, and is seen as the 'national river of Russia'. The river starts north-west of Moscow and flows out in to the Caspian Sea. Eleven out of the twenty largest cities of Russia, including its capital Moscow, are situated in the Volga basin. Over 40% of Russia's population live near it. It is used for transport, hydro-electric power production and irrigation. Some of the world's largest reservoirs can be found along its banks. It is a major source of Russia's water. The river plays a major part in the day to day life of the Russian people and is known as "Mother Volga".

Large quantities of wheat are grown in the fertile river valley, and an important petroleum industry is based in the Volga valley. Other minerals that are found include natural gas, salt, and potash, which is used as a fertiliser. The river's delta and the nearby Caspian Sea offer rich fishing grounds. The Volga also has a number of holiday destinations along its route, and many cruises take place along its course. Nearly the entire length of the River Volga is navigable from about March until mid-December.

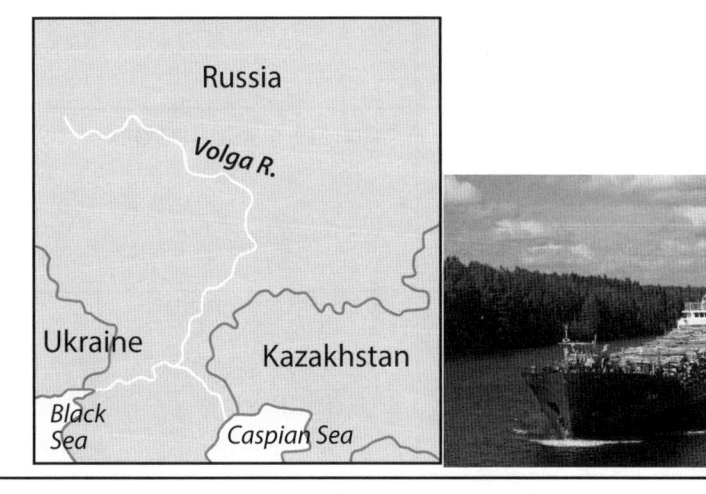

1 'Without the River Volga, Russia would not have become such a powerful country'. To what extent do you agree with this statement? Give reasons for your answer.

_____
_____
_____

2 What threats do you think the River Volga could be faced with? Give reasons for your answer.

_____
_____
_____

6.4 Russia's climate zones and biomes

Here you will find out more about Russia's varied climate and vegetation.

geog.3
pages 112–113

1. What is permafrost? What problems may this cause for people?

_____

_____

_____

2. Fill in the gaps in this table. Use the information on pages 112–113 in **geog.3** to help you.

Biome	Main features	Animals
	Covered in ice and snow in winter In summer the surface of the soil thaws	Musk ox, Arctic foxes, polar bears, grizzly bears, reindeer, ermine
Taiga		Bears, wolves, Siberian tigers
Temperate forest	Mixture of deciduous and coniferous trees	
		Cattle, hamsters, mice
Mountain		Mountain goats, deer, lynx and foxes

3. Which of the biomes would you like to visit? Give reasons for your answer.

_____

_____

_____

_____

_____

58   Russia

6.5 What about the people?

Here you will find out more about Russia's 146 million people.

pages 114–115

1 Why is the population denser in the European part of Russia?

_____

_____

2 Why are large areas of Siberia empty of people?

_____

_____

_____

3 Study pages 114 and 115 in **geog.3**. Link the numbers below to a fact about Russia's people. Write the facts in the space next to the number. The first one has been done to help you.

Number	Fact
1.2%	Percentage of Bakshirs, one of Russia's ethnic groups
74%	
5.0 million	
77%	
160	
146 million	
81%	

Russia 59

6.6 A tour of European Russia

Here you will explore Sochi, a tourist resort on the shores of the Black Sea.

geog.3
pages 116–117

- Sochi is the biggest resort town on what's called the "Russian Riviera"

- It is one of the few places in Russia with an almost subtropical climate, with warm to hot summers and mild winters

- You can enjoy glorious sunsets over the sea and admire the snow-capped mountains

- There are plenty of smart restaurants and outdoor cafes – Sochi has everything you could wish for in a resort

- Sochi has the backdrop of the Caucasus Mountains, pebble and sandy beaches and the ski resort is 30 miles away

- The average temperature is above 14 degrees Celsius, and the city boasts more than 200 days of sunshine a year

- Sochi, the host city of, and transformed by, the 2014 Winter Olympic Games, has turned into a year-round resort,

- Greater Sochi is the longest city in Europe – 146 km along the Black Sea Coast

- More than three million people visited Sochi during 2014 – a 28 per cent increase, year-on-year

- Over the New Year, more than 182,000 people visited the mountains, while 160,000 tourists spent time in Sochi

- Sochi: palm-fringed seaside resorts, spectacular ski facilities and a superb conference venue

1. Using the map and an atlas describe the location of Sochi. Remember to use geographical terms in your answer.

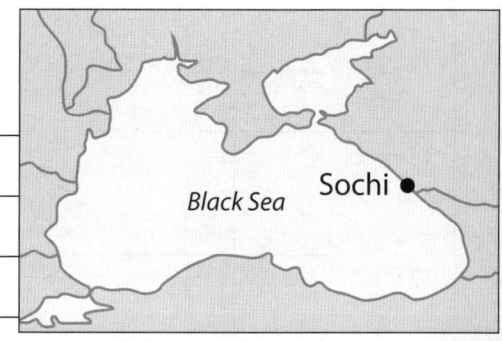

_____

_____

_____

Black Sea   Sochi ●

2. The Russian Prime Minister is expected to chair a conference on the development of tourist facilities and mountain skiing infrastructure in the Sochi area. You have been asked to prepare a 100 word news bulletin to help promote the resort. Use the information above to help you write your bulletin.

Remember to be persuasive!

_____

_____

_____

_____

_____

60   Russia

6.7 Sakha: Russia's biggest region

Here you will explore Sakha, Russia's coldest region.

pages 118–119

1. Look at the facts about Sakha below. Next to each, write one challenge that it would present for people.

Fact	**Challenge**
Russia's coldest region	_____
Ice roads are made across the River Lena	_____
Buildings are on concrete stilts	_____
The region is almost as big as India	_____
Many diamonds are mined	_____

2. Imagine you are visiting Yakutsk market in winter, as shown in the photograph. Write a tweet (remember, 140 characters maximum) to a friend in the UK describing your feelings.

_____
_____
_____
_____

3. Why might plans for Sakha's future cause problems for the region? Give reasons for your answer.

_____
_____
_____

Russia 61

6.8 So … how is Russia doing?

Here you will sum up what you know about Russia.

1 Complete the crossword below

Across
3 which party lost power?
7 biggest country by …
8 when people vote for their leaders
9 made famous by Bolshoi

Down
1 Russian currency
2 first animal in space
4 very wealthy Russians
5 percentage of Russians in poverty
6 gas is transported through these

'In terms of its geography, Russia is the most fortunate country on the planet'.

2 Do you agree or disagree with this statement? Give reasons for your answer.

_____
_____
_____
_____
_____
_____
_____

62 Russia

7 The Middle East

geog.3 pages 122–123

1 Write down two things that you already know about the Middle East.

   _____
   _____
   _____
   _____

2 This sail-shaped hotel in Dubai in the Middle East is 321 metres tall. Imagine that you are at the top. Using what you already know about the Middle East, label the photo to describe what you think you would see.

> Think about natural features and also those made or built by humans!

The Middle East 63

7.1 Introducing the Middle East

It's time to find out some facts about the Middle East.

1 Use the map on page 124 in **geog.3** to answer the following

   a If you travelled in a straight line from Cyprus to the border between Yemen and Oman, which countries would you pass through?

_____

   b Which two countries are found due south of Iraq?

_____

   c Which two countries lie south-east of Qatar?

_____

2 Write 'True' or 'False' in the box after each of these sentences.

   a The Middle East is where Asia, Europe and Africa meet.

   b The United Arab Emirates is made up of eight small states.

   c Yemen is an island nation.

   d The Middle East's large oil reserves are mainly in Egypt.

   e Islam is the dominant religion of the Middle East.

3 A region is an area that shares a feature – such as a distinct climate, or a language, or a mountain range. What do you think defines the Middle East as a region?

_____

_____

_____

_____

4 Research one country in the Middle East. Find out five fun facts and see if a partner can guess which country you have researched.

Fact 1 _____

Fact 2 _____

Fact 3 _____

Fact 4 _____

Fact 5 _____

The Middle East

7.2 The Middle East: physical geography

Here you will find out more about the Red Sea.

1 Read these facts about the Red Sea. Design a fact-filled poster that tells people what the Red Sea is like. You must include a map, and be as creative as you can!

- The region surrounding the Red Sea is one of the hottest, driest areas on the planet.
- The Red Sea is an extension of the Indian Ocean, located between Africa and Asia.
- It is around 190 miles across at its widest point, and about 1,200 miles long.
- Intense heat and little precipitation means the water in the Red Sea evaporates quickly.
- The Red Sea is home to over two hundred types of coral reefs.
- Water in the Red Sea has very clear visibility and warm temperatures throughout the year.
- It attracts divers, photographers, marine scientists, and tourists from all over the world.
- Cargo vessels, oil tankers, fishing boats, and cruise liners are all found sailing its waters.
- Desalination plants along its shores mean that its water can be purified for drinking.
- Sea water is also used for industry, such as cement works and oil refineries.
- 10% of fish species in the Red Sea are not found anywhere else on earth.
- Minerals build up in the Red Sea water as it evaporates so the sea is very saline, or salty.
- To the north, the Red Sea splits in two, the Gulf of Suez and the Gulf of Aqaba.
- The Suez Canal connects the Mediterranean Sea with the Red Sea's Gulf of Suez

The Middle East

7.3 The Middle East: climate zones and biomes

Here you will find out more about the Middle East's climate and vegetation.

geog.3
pages 128–129

1 The statements below explain why the Middle East does not get much rain. But they are in the wrong order! Write numbers in the table to show the correct order. Use page 128 in **geog.3** to help you.

Order	Climate fact
	It descends again at the Tropics, around 30° north and south of the Equator.
	Dry air means little or no rain.
	Heavy rain falls at the Equator.
	The land heats the air.
	The air cools, and its water vapour condenses.
	The warm air rises around the Equator.
	The risen air, which has lost all its moisture, gets pushed out of the way.
	The air is dry in the Middle East region.
	The land at the Equator gets hot.
	As the warm air rises, colder air moves in to take its place.

2 Circle the correct biome for the following sentences.

a	Bears and hyena are found here	Desert	Forest	Grassland
b	Plants may have spiky leaves	Desert	Forest	Grassland
c	Scorpions are found here	Desert	Forest	Grassland
d	Sometimes called Steppe	Desert	Forest	Grassland
e	A few trees may be found here	Desert	Forest	Grassland
f	Cypresses are found here	Desert	Forest	Grassland

3 Write fifteen words to explain how climate affects natural vegetation.

_____

_____

_____

The Middle East

7.4 The people of the Middle East

Here you will find out more about the Middle East's population.

geog.3
pages 130–131

1. Write down the correct answer at the end of each of these statements.

   a What is the combined population of Iraq and Iran to the nearest million?

   _____

   b Which country has a population almost exactly nine times bigger than Kuwait?

   _____

   c Which country has a population ten times bigger than London? _____

2. It is often said that 'Egypt is the gift of the Nile'. Explain what you think this means and how it has affected where Egypt's people live.

   _____
   _____
   _____

3. Who am I? Identify the two Middle Eastern countries from the facts given below.

I have five letters I am in the south I border the Red Sea I have a population of 26.7 million Answer _____	I am east of the Mediterranean Sea Kurds live in the north My capital is Tehran Most people speak Persian Answer _____

4. Middle East Challenge!

   Solve the word square below.

   arabs
   christian
   egypt
   iraq
   islam
   jews
   kurdistan
   kuwait
   lebanon
   mecca
   muslim
   oman
   qatar
   riyadh
   turkey

   ```
   h n n t e x i z o o c r r a p
   z a p a p u t l z y z z x t y
   y i m v t y n d h g w j e g a
   u t l v m s g f c u i u n j c
   r s e u r k i e y b q o o g v
   j i l a o b i d u j n t m c n
   e r y r l c b b r a m a l s i
   w h j a u i x e b u k j o z t
   s c z t d i r e k u k m y i u
   r c t a r h l a w y a t s o r
   c g k q j p f a q n g b r k k
   m e c c a s i f r x a g z l e
   l c a s w t n z m r v c k h y
   o m m l c k l n a f w q l h n
   j g u m u s l i m l v s k a a
   ```

The Middle East **67**

7.5 A closer look at the Arabian Peninsula

Here you will find out more about the world's biggest peninsula!

pages 132–133

1. Label the map below with the three facts about the Arabian Peninsula that you think are most significant or important.

Fact 1

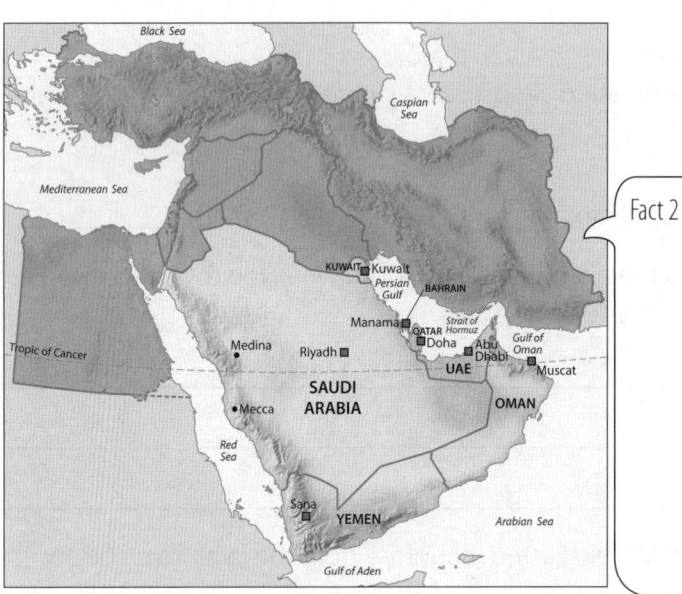

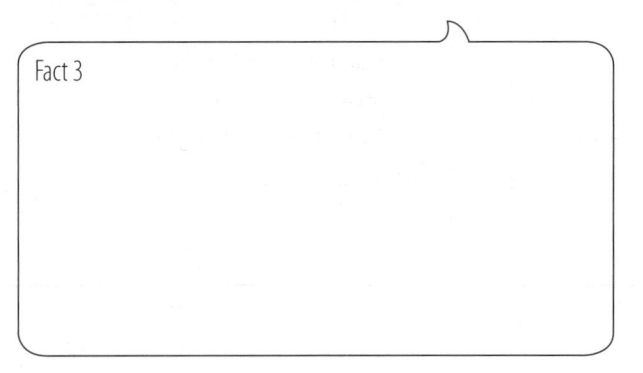

Fact 2

Fact 3

2. For each, explain why you think the fact is significant to either the region or the rest of the world.

I think Fact 1 is significant because… _____

_____

I think Fact 2 is significant because… _____

_____

I think Fact 3 is significant because… _____

_____

The Middle East

7.6 Conflict in the Middle East

Here you will find out some more about the conflicts found in the Middle East.

geog.3
pages 134–135

1. Conflict always leads to people becoming refugees. What do you think a refugee is?

_____

_____

> **Over 5 million children** in **Syria** need **emergency help**.
>
> **1 million** of these children **have fled** to neighbouring countries **in search of safety**.
>
> **1 in 3** of these children have been **hit**, **kicked**, or **shot at**.
>
> **7000** innocent children have been **killed**.

2. The information about children in Syria above was taken from the website of the British charity, Save the Children, in 2015.

Look at some support options given in the table below and rank them 1–5 with number 1 being, in your view, the most urgent.

RANK	Type of Support
	Provide nutritious food for Syrian children
	Offer permanent resettlement to families in other countries
	Provide doctors
	Support education in Syrian refugee camps
	Provide clean water to refugee camps

3. Explain in detail why you have chosen your number 1. Why do you think it will best support Syrian children through this crisis?

_____

_____

_____

_____

_____

_____

The Middle East 69

7.7 Israel and the State of Palestine

Here you will find out some more about Palestine and its problems.

pages 136–137

1. Why does Gaza say it is being 'strangled'?

2. How do you think Gaza copes with this, and what problems may it cause its people in their everyday lives?

3. Jerusalem faces many problems. Choose three and summarise them in your own words.

   Jerusalem's problems

   a

   b

   c

4. The Israeli Ministry of Tourism describes Jerusalem as *'a city of overwhelming emotions, a city that promises a religious and spiritual experience, excitement and pleasure, interesting tours and entertaining adventures.'*

   Would you like to visit Jerusalem? Give reasons for your answer.

   YES / NO (please circle)

70 The Middle East